GALE
CENGAGE Learning

Short Stories for Students, Volume 46

Project Editor: Kristen A. Dorsch Rights Acquisition and Management: Ashley Maynard Composition: Evi Abou-El-Seoud

Manufacturing: Rita Wimberley

Imaging: John Watkins

Product Design: Pamela A. E. Galbreath, Jennifer Wahi Digital Content Production: Edna Shy © 2018 Gale, A Cengage Company

Gale
27500 Drake Rd.
Farmington Hills, MI, 48331-3535

ISBN-13: 978-1-4103-2858-8
ISSN 1092-7735

This title is also available as an e-book.
ISBN-13: 978-1-4103-2863-2
Contact your Gale, A Cengage Company sales

representative for ordering information.

Printed in Mexico
1 2 3 4 5 6 7 21 20 19 18 17

All Summer in a Day

Ray Bradbury

1954

Introduction

Ray Bradbury's "All Summer in a Day" was first published, as were many of his tales, in *Fantasy & Science Fiction Magazine*, appearing in the March 1954 issue. It was collected in *A Medicine for Melancholy and Other Stories* in 1959 and appears in other Bradbury collections.

Bradbury's career had three periods: early, classic, and late. The early-period weird tales were written before his twenty-sixth year and collected in *Dark Carnival* (1947). The classic science fiction period, from 1946 to 1955, that made Bradbury famous includes *A Medicine for Melancholy, The Martian Chronicles, The Illustrated Man, The Golden Apples of the Sun,* and *Fahrenheit 451.* In the late period, which began in 1957 with *Dandelion Wine,* Bradbury tried to show the redeeming and happy side of human nature, but he did not stop writing about dark subjects. He considered himself mostly a fantasist and believed only *Fahrenheit 451* could strictly be called science fiction.

"All Summer in a Day" is a seemingly simple tale about a class of children doing a science project on the planet Venus. It is set in the future when Americans have settled a colony there. The premise of the story is that on Venus the sun appears for only two hours every seven years and the children await this astronomical wonder as if they await a comet or eclipse. The story, however, has depth and can be read mythically or allegorically as yielding a lesson about human behavior.

Author Biography

Bradbury was born on August 22, 1920, in Waukegan, Illinois, to Leonard Spaulding Bradbury, a telephone lineman, and Esther Moberg Bradbury. Bradbury claimed that he had total recall from birth, and perhaps for this reason, he was gifted at writing about the life of children. He had three siblings, two of whom died in childhood. Bradbury's family moved to Los Angeles in 1934, and he graduated from Los Angeles High School in 1938. Bradbury had a painful adolescence because he was not athletic and outgoing but was an imaginative bookworm. In this he is a little like Margot in "All Summer in a Day."

Bradbury did not go to college because his parents could not afford it. He educated himself by reading in libraries. As a child, he read comics, pulp magazines like *Amazing Stories*, Edgar Allan Poe, L. Frank Baum, fairy tales, Edgar Rice Burroughs, H. G. Wells, and Jules Verne. He began writing stories when he was twelve.

He was fascinated with traveling circuses and appeared on stage as a volunteer with Blackstone the Magician in 1931. He once attended a writing class taught by the science fiction writer Robert Heinlein, and at the age of fifteen he began submitting his work to magazines. He joined the Los Angeles Science Fiction League in 1937. The league's magazine, *Imagination!*, in 1938 was the first to print a Bradbury short story. In 1942, Bradbury sold stories to *Weird Tales*, a dark fantasy magazine.

Bradbury's first collected work, *Dark Carnival* (1947), was published by Arkham House, the publisher of the horror master H. P. Lovecraft. In 1947, Bradbury married Maggie McClure and began his family of four children. Influenced by Thomas Wolfe, Poe, Sherwood Anderson, and other American writers, Bradbury became known as a poetic stylist and began to publish in more mainstream magazines such as *Harper's* and the *New Yorker*.

Bradbury's fame was assured in 1950 when *The Martian Chronicles* (1950) placed not only him but also fantasy and science fiction in mainstream literature. The book was enthusiastically received by critics. *The Martian Chronicles, The Illustrated Man* (1951), and *Fahrenheit 451* (1953) were called science fiction, but Bradbury's style involved more literary symbolism than hard science. Even though Bradbury was excited about space exploration, in his work he was critical of technology, believing that technology had destroyed civilization.

Bradbury branched out to write screenplays, such as *It Came from Outer Space* (1953) and *Moby Dick* (1956), and television scripts, including episodes of *The Alfred Hitchcock Hour, Alfred Hitchcock Presents*, and Rod Serling's *The Twilight Zone. Dandelion Wine* (1957) was Bradbury's first collection of stories about Green Town, Illinois, based on his boyhood in Waukegan. "All Summer in a Day" was published in his collection *A Medicine for Melancholy and Other Stories* in 1959. His first novel, *Something Wicked This Way Comes* (1962) also dealt with Green Town but with a different set of characters. This story was made into a Disney film with Bradbury's film script in 1983.

Bradbury died on June 5, 2012, in Los Angeles, at the age of ninety-one, after a lengthy illness following a stroke in 1999. He published over five hundred works, including short stories, novels, poetry, screenplays, television scripts, stage plays, and essays. He was most famous for science fiction and fantasy but also wrote mysteries, realistic social fiction, and nostalgic small-town idylls. He won a World Fantasy Award for Lifetime Achievement in 1977. He also won the Gandalf, PEN, and National Book Foundation awards, the Grand Master Nebula Award (1988), the Bram Stoker Award for Lifetime Achievement (1988), and numerous Science Fiction and Fantasy Writers of America awards.

Plot Summary

The children are pressing their faces to the windows at school and asking, will it really happen today? They live on Venus, where it has rained continuously for seven years, producing lush forests, swamps, and the constant sound of gushing water and tidal waves smashing everything to the ground. These are the children of the space explorers who came to Venus to set up a new civilization. They are nine years old and are waiting for the sun to appear, as it does once every seven years for an hour or two. The last time it shone, they were too young to remember, but Margot remembers, because she has come to Venus later than the others and remembers the sun of Earth. A day earlier, in anticipation of the event, the children wrote stories about the sun, and Margot read her poem comparing the sun to a flower that blooms for only an hour.

Margot is very frail and different from the other children, because she suffers from the lack of sun. She is ghostly and washed out and does not play with the others. She came from Ohio when she was four years old and speaks of the sun to the other children. They do not believe anything she says, and one boy, William, shoves her and mocks her. She is passive. The other children hate her because she is different. There is talk that her parents are taking her back to Earth, though this will mean a loss of income for them. Margot does not accept or thrive on Venus. Perhaps the others are jealous of her possible future. They tease her for standing at the window waiting for the sun to appear. They tell her it will not come, but she insists the scientists predicted that it would appear this day. William leads the crowd of children in taunts, insisting that they put Margot in the closet before the teacher returns. Though Margot struggles, they lock her in. She cries and beats on the door to be let out.

Media Adaptations

- The 1982 video adaptation of "All Summer in a Day," by Learning Corporation of America, emphasizes William's cruelty and Margot's forgiveness. The script is by S. Murdock Donaldson and the direction by Ed Kaplan. The producer is Karl Epstein. The video is twenty-six minutes long and available at https://www.youtube.com/watch?v=cV-rz Gx21rw via YouTube.

- An audiobook of "All Summer in a Day" read by Justin Franco, uploaded on July 3, 2014, is available at https://www.youtube.com/watch?v=SaLzm3B1ewY via YouTube. The reading runs eleven minutes and forty seconds.

- A brief animation of "All Summer in a Day" made by Brianna Paz using Powtoon, produced by Paz2969, and uploaded on July 20, 2015, is available at https://www.youtube.com/watch?v=wwkLV7zgiKs via YouTube. The run time is two minutes and thirty-six seconds.

The teacher returns and ushers the children to the door to look outside. They suddenly hear silence replace the constant roaring of storm. They look out as the rain stops. The sun comes out blazing in the tropical landscape. The teacher warns them they have only two hours, but the children hardly hear her, for they are running and shouting in the sun. There is no green, however, for they are in a great jungle of gray, rubber-like plants. There is no greening from chlorophyll. They run and play, but mostly they stare at the sun and breathe fresh air. Finally, someone feels a drop of rain start again, and all the children begin to moan as the wind starts up and thunder crashes, sending them to their underground buildings. As they hear the roar of the storms start up again, they ask if it will be seven more years before the sun comes again. The teacher says yes. Suddenly, one child remembers Margot is still in the closet. The children are solemn, ashamed, and cannot look at one another. They go to the closet. It is quiet. They open the door and let Margot out.

Characters

Children

The children in the science class on Venus are nine years old. They are together in their class waiting for the sun to appear, as scientists have predicted. They are compared to roses or intermixed weeds pressing their faces to the glass to look out at the endless rain. These metaphors establish the situation of these children of Venus pioneers. First, they are roses waiting for the sun to bloom. Second, they are weeds because they have been stunted by the climate on Venus. They are intermixed, meaning they are different types. Weeds grow in wild places; sometimes they are beneficial and sometimes obnoxious, like William. They are not cultivated so they grow however they can. This is the fate of these children, who are not as refined in their behavior and sensibility as Margot is, because they have forgotten the sun. As part of their science lesson, they are waiting for the sun to appear, as it does once every seven years.

The children are also compared to a wheel that turns back on itself when they turn into the mob that goes after Margot to lock her in the closet. The wheel image implies something that crushes and cannot stop once in motion. The rain is also said to crush everything on the planet; it is implied that the climate has made the children mean. Margot is not part of the wheel, this group of Venus-grown children who are alike but different from the Earth girl. Once they are released for an hour in the sun, the children are compared to animals released from cages, romping in joy. The sun gives life and energy to them. They become civilized and repent of their treatment of Margot after their time romping in the sun.

Margot

Margot is a loner. She is different from the other nine-year-old children because she did not move to Venus until she was four. She grew up in Ohio and remembers the sun. She is interested only in sun, and the other children do not know what she is talking about. They accuse her of lying. She has ostracized herself from the other children; she plays no games with them in the underground tunnels that serve as the buildings on Venus. She is described as having been lost in or washed out by the rain. There is hardly any of her left. She is colorless, pale, and frail, like an old photograph. She is a ghost, barely surviving. The vegetation of Venus is described as similarly washed out and deprived of color. It is like rubber, the color of ash or white cheese. Margot's parents are rumored to be considering taking her back to Earth, so they must be worried about her. Obviously depressed, she allows William to bully her, not even defending herself.

The story hints that Margot is a sensitive, artistic type who feeds on beauty. Here she is deprived of natural beauty. She writes a poem about the sun, and the other children do not believe she is capable of it. It is implied that the trauma Margot undergoes imprisoned in the dark closet while the sun is out is beyond words. When the children return, her cries have ceased. There is only silence and dark. In some way, they have killed her spirit, even if her body survives.

Teacher

The teacher is not given any personality but seems inept. She is out of the room when the children do their evil. She does not even notice Margot's absence. Bradbury often views adults from a child's point of view, and in this case, adults, even teachers, do not have individuality but only represent an authority figure. The children have their own independent society apart from adults. The teacher lamely rebukes William for doubting Margot's poem. She is no ally for the hapless child and is not capable of protecting her.

William

William is a cruel boy. He not only physically bullies Margot but also torments her psychologically by refusing to believe there is a sun or that it will appear. He undermines her faith and hope and persuades the other children to follow him. He tries to make her feel she is crazy by denying her truth. William is the kind of aggressive leader who can use the weakness of others to put himself forward and gain a following. He convinces the other children that there is something wrong with Margot and that this means they are better than she is. They punish her for her difference instead of feeling sympathy for her plight or offering her their friendship and support. William feels a sense of power by using Margot as a scapegoat. The others follow him. He excuses locking her in a closet as a prank instead of the torture and abuse it represents.

Society sometimes tolerates nasty behavior of children as simply mischievous, but Bradbury shows that the tendency of good and evil is present even in the young. A normal, loving child William's age would not have locked a suffering, weak girl in a closet and deprived her of the only thing she lives for. William not only is cruel to Margot but also rallies the other children to commit evil against her. They all lie to the teacher when she asks if everyone is there. Yet William is not hopeless; he learns from the event and even feels remorse. This shows he is capable of growth, even though it may be too late for Margot.

Extraterrestrial Life

"All Summer in a Day" is one of Bradbury's science fiction stories set on Venus. Although no Venusians are pictured, the planet is presented as a jungle with constant storms and incessant rain. The Earth people who have settled there have had to build underground dwellings for protection from violent storms and tidal waves. Bradbury's overall philosophy of space travel is that it represents human desire for greater vistas. In this story, however, he shows a dystopia in which the humans are locked up in a hostile environment, causing them to behave toward one another in a stunted way. The children who are born there have never seen the sun on Earth. They don't know the freedom of playing outside in nature. Furthermore, they have no tolerance of anyone, like Margot, who remembers the sun on Earth. They do not believe Margot's tales about the sun or that it is possible for her to write a poem about it.

Bradbury wrote this story when it was still assumed that Venus was a wet planet because from Earth it appears covered by clouds. The effectiveness of the story is not in its factual details of an alien environment but in imagining the result of living in a climate so inhospitable and unlike that of Earth. Bradbury speculates on the sort of character building a planet represents, thus appreciating the beauty and freedom Earth life has given to humans. The sun, for instance, gives not only life but also a sense of freedom. Margot is declining with lack of exposure to the sun. Ecopsychologists have found that nature affects the mental health of humans. Margot is weak and cannot stand up for herself. Being shut in the closet is a symbol of what her life has been like on Venus. She has no ability to interact with the children who have lived without her reference point, the sun. The story illustrates the centrality of the sun to those on Earth, something taken for granted. On Venus, the sun appears once every seven years for one or two hours and seems like a miracle.

Childhood

Because Bradbury remembered his own childhood so vividly, he often portrayed childhood in his fiction. It is a favorite theme. "All Summer in a Day" shows both sides of childhood—its pain and its sense of freedom. Margot is subjected to bullying and abuse by the other children. Adults cannot always be there to protect, and in this case, the teacher is out of the room. She has also forgotten Margot in the excitement of the event taking place. Margot is alone and neglected, abused. This is one of the cruelties and injustices of childhood that many people experience. Margot also represents the marginalized person in a culture that has a different perspective or truth. She believes in the sun and talks about it; the other children, perhaps out of envy, reject her reality. It is also rumored that her parents may take her back to Earth. She appears to have more options for the future than they do. The joy of childhood, on the other hand, is represented by the children let loose to enjoy the sun for two hours. This sudden happiness is overwhelming. They frolic in the ugly vegetation as though in a garden. They change and open up, shouting and playing like regular children on a summer's day. It is the first time they can remember not hearing the constant roaring of storm. The silence and sun act as an elixir.

Stories about childhood often contrast imprisonment and freedom as they affect the nature of children. Charlotte Brontë's *Jane Eyre*, for instance, contains the red room incident in which Jane is locked up as punishment and faints from fear. William Wordsworth romanticized childhood and spoke of school as a prison, suggesting that a boy could learn more from rambling free in nature. Wordsworth claimed that it was nature that taught the moral lessons of life to humans. No wonder the children on Venus are mean. They are never outdoors in a benign environment.

Topics for Further Study

- Write a science fiction story set on another planet or in another solar system. Decide whether you want to write hard science fiction based on speculation from known scientific law or fantastic science fiction based on imagination, as in Bradbury's story. If you need to research a scientific question, do it and present the facts in your story. Read the stories in a group, discussing the diversity and flexibility of the sci-fi genre.

- Write a short critical paper on your favorite science fiction writer, citing one or more works. Include quotes and examples of your main point about why this is good science fiction. How does it teach you about science, expand your vistas, or seem to solve a social or technological problem?

- Read the young-adult novel *The Dragonriders of Pern* (1967), by Anne McCaffrey, the first woman to win a Hugo Award and also the first woman to receive a Nebula Award. This is the first of a series of twenty-two novels. Pern is a preindustrial society that uses dragons with telepathic riders to fight their enemy, Thread, a destructive spore from a rogue planet. As a class, discuss what the reader can learn about human behavior by looking at a fictitious alien society. After the discussion, ask each participant to write and hand in a reading journal entry on the subject.

- In a group, prepare a slide presentation on the history of NASA, the US National Aeronautic and Space Administration, including its missions and accomplishments. Assign each participant or small group a mission and have them describe its technological features and the information about space it collected. Conclude with an evaluation of NASA's importance to scientific knowledge and the possibilities for future missions to the moon and Mars.

- Construct a group website on the role science fiction can play in promoting racial and social tolerance. Find sci-fi stories written by Americans of various ethnic backgrounds and religions and by authors outside the United States and highlight their special angles and social messages. Often, space stories picture astronauts from different cultures cooperating in space, as on the International Space Station. Write a short plot summary of each story, background on the author, and any important lesson in international or interspecies cooperation.

Good and Evil

Bradbury is a moral fabulist. His mythic style of storytelling frequently focuses on good and evil as a theme. Humans can be both and can choose one or the other. In the beginning, the children, perhaps conditioned by the gloom of Venus with its constant wind and storm, are cruel to Margot. They commit an act of violence, locking her in the closet, depriving her of freedom and of the thing she most desires, to see the sun. The narrator has built up the tension to show that Margot is not doing well. She is frail from lack of exposure to the sun. This rare glimpse of the sun on Venus every seven years is not just an adventure for her as it is for the other children. It is life or death for her physical health and certainly for her mental health. She is the only child who really believes in the sun, and because of evil and envy, the other children, led by William, want to punish her for her belief in the light. They want to prove her wrong by putting her in the dark. The sun thus symbolizes goodness in human nature, whereas the storm symbolizes the dark and evil. The children approach the closet without looking at one another. They feel guilt, for they can anticipate that the quiet in the closet means Margot has died. They have killed the life and hope in her.

Science Fiction

Bradbury got his start as a science fiction writer and in the 1950s was considered the most famous science fiction writer in the United States for such books as *The Martian Chronicles* and *Fahrenheit 451* and many short stories. "All Summer in a Day" was published at the height of this fame. His reputation later changed as science fiction writers dedicated to hard science replaced the popularity of Bradbury's more mythic emphasis. For instance, the only thing that makes "All Summer in a Day" science fiction is that it is about imagined life on a Venus populated by space settlers. It does not use scientific data to enhance the story and make it seem more real. In reality, Venus is a scorching hot planet. In the story, there are no details about how the settlers made the underground shelters or about the physics of the planet and weather systems. This aspect is subordinate to the idea of life on Venus. Bradbury considered science fiction a fiction of ideas, not of facts.

Space travel and life on other planets allowed the author to explore questions about human nature much as pioneer and wilderness stories show humans confronting basic moral and survival issues. This makes Bradbury's science fiction more like that of C. S. Lewis in *Perelandra: Voyage to Venus*

(1943) rather than that of Isaac Asimov in *Foundation* (1951), in which the author extrapolated on real scientific law.

Biblical Myth and Symbol

Bradbury was not religious, as was C. S. Lewis, but he did have a somewhat mystical view of life that is expressed in passages of poetic wonder. He appreciated myth and symbol and authors who used these techniques, especially the gothic writers, Poe, Nathaniel Hawthorne, and Herman Melville. Though they portrayed the dark side, these authors relied on spiritual symbols and biblical myth. Similarly, Bradbury makes an allegory of his story about Venus. Light and dark symbolize good and evil. The space voyagers have not made an Eden of Venus but rather live in a fallen world with plants that are like rubber, the color of ash.

There is no inner or outer beauty. Margot's poem is mocked. These humans are not on Venus to perfect society or life but to make money. Margot's parents might have to take her back to Earth, but it is mentioned that they will lose thousands of dollars in pay if they leave.

Bradbury often uses seasons and weather as symbols. Summer is brief on Venus, only a few hours. Summer in Bradbury's Green Town stories, exemplified in *Dandelion Wine* (1957), symbolizes a state of innocence and fullness of life. In "All Summer in a Day," summer is almost nonexistent, and the children are not innocent. The children are allowed to taste summer briefly and are visibly changed by the sun as it appears on their desolate world. They run and shout until they feel the rain begin again, and they are escorted underground once more. Storms, like the permanent one on Venus, come from the evil forces in Bradbury's usual mythic formula. This storm is not just rain but violence and disturbance, a constant flood and roaring wind, like living inside a cyclone. The sun awakens the conscience of the children to realize their cruelty to Margot. She still has the sun inside her and can make a poem about it until she is locked in the dark closet. Bradbury makes Margot's relationship with the sun seem like a religious one.

Poetry and Verbal Music

Though he was a writer of horror stories and science fiction, Bradbury is noted for his lush style, full of vivid imagery, music, and color. His poetic language can sometimes develop a metaphor into prolonged and breathless purple prose (ornate and elaborate language), similar to that of Melville or Thomas Wolfe. On the other hand, he also admired the compression and minimalism of Ernest Hemingway, sometimes going to the other extreme in style. In "All Summer in a Day," the directness of action and dialogue more resembles Hemingway's style. But Bradbury's forte of poetic description shows in his picture of the eternal rain and, by contrast, Margot's inner point of view, her dreams and memories of sun.

The length of the story is in keeping with Bradbury's preference for poetry and short stories, the vivid and emotional vignettes that make an impression. Even some of his novels, such as *The Martian Chronicles* and *Dandelion Wine*, are actually short-story cycles, many short stories assembled as moments highlighted for similar thematic resonance. In this story, Bradbury appeals to the senses with the loud sound of the storm and the sudden silence of the sun, with the washed-out drabness of the landscape and the warmth and color of sunlight. These sensory images make Margot's fate in the dark closet seem more horrible. She is so sensitive that she has covered her ears and refused to take a shower because its noise sounds like the storm. She is an artist by temperament, the only child who can write a poem about the sun. Margot believes the other children have an innate memory of sun in them that they dream as they sleep. Bradbury's poetic treatment of his parable about light and dark makes it all the more memorable. The contrast between storm and sun is stark, like a brilliant watercolor painting of few strokes.

Science Fiction

Stories about space travel to the moon and stars go back to ancient cultures, but such stories would not be possible without scientific discoveries. Nicolaus Copernicus challenged the religious doctrine of the Catholic Church with his discovery that Earth and the other planets rotate around the sun, the beginning of modern understanding of the solar system. Giordano Bruno was burned at the stake in 1600 for saying that the universe was infinite and contained many worlds. Before the scientific revolution, facts were not necessary or appreciated because stories about travel beyond Earth took place in a fixed and divine realm, such as that of Dante's *Divine Comedy* (c. 1307). Science and the fiction it inspired rose together and cross-pollinated, scientists often writing fiction or developing their scientific ideas in fiction. Johannes Kepler was an astronomer who discovered laws of planetary motion that he included in his fiction, *Somnium*, a journey to the moon. Writers used the discoveries of the laws of motion by Sir Isaac Newton, for instance, to imagine travel to other worlds in the genre called *voyages extraordinaires*, which included Voltaire's *Micromégas* (1752), about a giant alien.

Modern science fiction was born with Mary

Shelley's *Frankenstein* (1818). Frankenstein is a scientist who makes human life in the laboratory, though Shelley does not say how he does it. Later, galvanism and electricity were supplied as the explanation. Edgar Allan Poe's "The Unparalleled Adventure of One Hans Pfaall" (1835) uses Kepler's ideas about going to the moon. Jules Verne made science fiction a popular genre in the nineteenth century with his *voyages extraordinaires*, which tried to give a sense of scientific realism with ideas about rockets and submarines in *From the Earth to the Moon* (1865) and *Twenty Thousand Leagues Under the Sea* (1870). H. G. Wells had even more influence on the genre as a student of Darwinian evolution and the ideas of the biologist Thomas Huxley. His masterpieces include *The Time Machine* (1895), *The Invisible Man* (1897), *The War of the Worlds* (1898), and *The First Men in the Moon* (1901). Wells used science fiction to comment on social problems, as Bradbury did.

Compare & Contrast

- **1959:** The space race to the moon is initiated during the Cold War between the United States and the Soviet Union.
  Today: The International Space Station is run by astronauts from many countries cooperating in scientific experiments.

- **1959:** Governments with large

budgets and resources are the only institutions able to do space research.

Today: Private enterprise, such as the company SpaceX, contributes to space research with reusable rockets and other inventions.

- **1959:** Science fiction records the human desire to find life on other planets, imagining there may be livable planets in the solar system, such as Mars and Venus.

  Today: NASA announces the discovery of exoplanets, seven rocky planets of Earth size beyond the solar system, in orbit around a star called Trappist-1, which may be livable.

Bradbury was also influenced by the high modernist science fiction writers of the twentieth century with their humanist fears about machines taking over, such as Aldous Huxley in *Brave New World* (1932) and George Orwell in *1984* (1949). As a boy and a teen, Bradbury was inspired by the pulp science fiction of Edgar Rice Burroughs and his Martian journeys. The 1930s was also a time when comic books produced the space heroes Buck Rogers and Flash Gordon. Superheroes like Superman came from outer space with special powers. Bradbury began to publish science fiction stories in magazines as a teen and came to prominence in the golden age of science fiction, 1940– 1960, with *The Martian Chronicles* (1950) and *Fahrenheit 451* (1953). He shared the limelight with Isaac Asimov, whose *Foundation* series starting in 1951 was credited as an important switch to hard science fiction based on fact and the solving of problems. Other giants of the era were Robert A. Heinlein with *The Puppet Masters* (1951) and Arthur C. Clarke with *Childhood's End* (1953). At this point science fiction was a form of speculative fiction without hard boundaries and often blurred with fantasy. As fantasy and science fiction began to take different trajectories, many saw Bradbury as more fantasist and Asimov as the true science fiction writer.

The launching of *Sputnik* by the Soviet Union in 1957 began a space race with the United States that simultaneously inspired a more sophisticated science fiction. Frank Herbert's *Dune* series starting in 1965 included complex physics, drugs, race, religion, and politics. Philip K. Dick's *Do Androids Dream of Electric Sheep?* (1968), the plot for the film *Blade Runner* (1982), pictures a desolate Earth where it is difficult to distinguish humans and androids. Ursula Le Guin added a feminist perspective with *The Left Hand of Darkness* (1969), about a planet without fixed gender roles.

From 1960 to 2000, science fiction became a blockbuster visual medium with special effects in the films *2001: A Space Odyssey* (1968), *Star Wars* (1977), *Mad Max* (1979), *Star Trek* (1979), *E. T: The Extra-Terrestrial* (1982), *The Matrix* (1999), and others. Science fiction had become more specific and realistic in terms of science because of technological advances. Contemporary stories dealt with virtual reality, computers, and scenarios based on actual space travel and spacecraft, sometimes trying to solve real space problems, as in the novel *The Martian* (2011), by Andy Weir, which was made into a film in 2015 and was based on existing technology and consultations with NASA engineers.

Space Travel

For over fifty years, the Soviet Union and the United States poured resources into space research, an initiative dedicated not only to pure science but also to the politics of the Cold War. The space race, from the moment the Soviets launched the satellite *Sputnik* in 1957, had the goal of putting the first man on the moon to demonstrate superior science. The United States did so, however, in the summer of 1969 with the first Apollo lunar landing. Space technology was deemed important for nuclear warhead capability in the arms race. NASA was established in 1958 to oversee the major space initiatives of the United States. In the early twenty-first century, the countries involved in space exploration included Russia, Ukraine, Japan, India, and China, in addition to the United States and the various members of the European Space Agency.

The Soviet Union accomplished many important firsts in space, including the first satellite, the first human to orbit Earth, the first space-walk, and the first launch to Mars, in 1962. In the 1970s, the Soviet Union sent the first probes to Venus and Mars that finally brought back data on the planets that had been most popular in science fiction. The United States put the first human on the moon and launched the International Space Station, which has been inhabited by astronauts from all over the world since 2000. The Hubble Space Telescope, launched in 1990; the Chandra X-ray telescope, in 1999; and the Kepler Space Observatory, in 2009, to look for Earth-like planets, have vastly extended scientific knowledge of space. The Mars rover *Sojourner* landed on Mars in 1997 to collect and bring back data from the planet that is on NASA's list to conquer in the near future.

Bradbury told the story that he stayed up all night with Carl Sagan to watch the *Viking 1* landing on Mars on July 20, 1976. The scientists and science fiction writers were equally interested, for stories about Mars were different before and after space exploration. Previously, Mars was thought to have vegetation because of the color changes there, and there was speculation about a civilization with aliens called Martians, as in Bradbury's *Martian Chronicles*. Mars turned out to be a very cold, uninhabited planet with a thin atmosphere of carbon dioxide. It might have had water once but was found to have none and to be incapable of supporting human life. It is pounded by dust storms. Similarly, stories of Venus became different after space exploration.

The old Venus of science fiction in the 1960s

and before was imagined to be very wet from the cloud cover that does not allow the surface to be seen. Bradbury played with this fact by having Venus lashed with constant thunderstorms and consisting of a dark swampy landscape with the sun rarely appearing. There is an ashen light on the dark side of Venus that Bradbury refers to as the color of the vegetation. The new Venus after the *Venera* space probes in 1975 and 1982 showed Venus to be a complete surprise. The clouds were found to be sulfuric acid and the surface temperature so hot it could melt lead. The dry desert, volcanic activity, and lightning storms make the name of this planet, after the Roman goddess of love and beauty, ironic. Scientists came to refer to Venus as Earth's evil twin because of its hellish landscape and extremely dense atmosphere of carbon dioxide. It might once have had water but is an example of the greenhouse effect that makes a planet uninhabitable.

Critical Overview

"All Summer in a Day" was published in 1954 in *Fantasy & Science Fiction Magazine* and collected in 1959 in the volume *A Medicine for Melancholy and Other Stories*. The collection came out at a time of heightened interest in science fiction during the Cold War after the launching of the Soviet satellite *Sputnik* in 1957. Critics were already noticing that Bradbury's science fiction was not like the hard science stories of Isaac Asimov. Bradbury had become a popular pulp magazine science fiction writer in the 1940s and one of the most famous American science fiction writers of the 1940s and 1950s. Critics at first were thrilled that his more literary style contrasted with the many science fiction writers who only emphasized weird ideas and inventions. Christopher Isherwood was one of the prominent critics who fostered Bradbury's elevation as an important writer. In his review of *The Martian Chronicles* in *Tomorrow* magazine in October 1950, Isherwood identified the book as better than mere science fiction; it was part of a fantasy tradition going back to Poe. Isherwood understood that Bradbury's space stories were important parables written in a beautiful language.

Within the next three years, Bradbury produced his most famous work besides *The Martian Chronicles*: *The Illustrated Man*, "It Came from Outer Space," and *Fahrenheit 451*. Angus Wilson, in a review of *Fahrenheit 451* for *Science*

Fiction News in the spring of 1953, wrote that the book was a contribution to mainstream American fiction. J. B. Priestley, in the article "They Came from Inner Space" in the *New Statesman and Nation* in 1953, called Bradbury a new kind of science fiction writer with imagination and literary worth. Orville Prescott, in a 1953 *New York Times* review of *Fahrenheit 451*, called Bradbury "the uncrowned king of the science fiction writers."

A trend that began with Edward Wood's piece in the first issue of the *Journal of Science Fiction* in 1951, however, claimed that Bradbury might have been a brilliant writer but that he was not writing science fiction. Until that time, science fiction did not have its own standards or critical parameters. The science fiction writers Damon Knight and James Blish began to establish standards by which they judged Bradbury as deficient. They determined that science fiction was extrapolation on known science. In his 1964 book *The Issue at Hand*, Blish (William Atheling Jr.) claimed that Bradbury's writing style was ruining the field of science fiction. Knight, in the 1967 update of his book *In Search of Wonder: Essays on Modern Science Fiction*, first published in 1956, called Bradbury's writing anti–science fiction because of Bradbury's distrust of science.

Bradbury's popularity never suffered with the public, but many readers resented his role as the representative of science fiction. His fans claimed that his mythic and humanistic fables were in the tradition of such science fiction writers as H. G.

Wells, Aldous Huxley, and Ursula Le Guin. The argument has never been settled; some readers prefer more hard science, and some prefer the fantastic.

In *The History of Science Fiction* (2006), Adam Roberts classified Bradbury with religious science fiction writers. According to Roberts, Bradbury was leading a strand of science fiction that uses religious ideas and myths. Roberts found theological love to be the core of Bradbury's ethic, even in outer space. This is illustrated in "All Summer in a Day" with the children's cruel treatment of Margot when she needs love and understanding. Roberts comments, "There is this blending of nostalgic solace and childhood night terrors in all Bradbury's best work; certainties evaporate, and alienness is simultaneously externalised and internalised." Roberts also finds in Bradbury "an almost millenarian yearning for escape." Instead of focusing on a weird alien of Venus, Bradbury explores alienness with Margot as the unexpected alien exposed to scorn. Instead of glamorizing space travel, Bradbury shows that there is a lack of love and charity in human life.

What Do I Read Next?

- Bradbury's *The Martian Chronicles* (1950) was hailed as a major work of science fiction in its day, though it does not resemble later hard science fiction. This collection of short stories shows the conflict between the telepathic Venusians and the hard-headed colonizers that suggests the conflict between pioneers and Indians in the American Old West. *The Martian Chronicles* is a satire on American colonial mentality.

- Edgar Rice Burroughs was a favorite author of Bradbury's, and his Venus books inspired Bradbury's own stories about Venus. *Carson of Venus*, third in a series, came out in

1939 and became immediately important for its political satire on Nazi Germany and Benito Mussolini's fascism. Bradbury also learned to combine space fantasy with satire and fable.

- Shinichi Hoshi is Japan's most famous science fiction writer. His story "Bokko-chan," translated into English and published in the *Magazine of Fantasy and Science Fiction* in June 1963, is about a supposed female bartender who is really a robot. The story comments on the rigidity of female roles in Japan at that time.

- Madeleine L'Engle's *A Swiftly Tilting Planet*, published in 1978, is a young-adult science fiction story about using time travel and telepathy to prevent nuclear war.

- *Old Venus* (2015), edited by George R. R. Martin and Gardner Dozois, is a collection of retro science fiction stories written by seventeen contemporary authors in the style of the pulp magazines of the 1960s. The editors are two giants in the world of science fiction. Authors including Allan M. Steele, Lavie Tildar, Paul McAuley, Matthew Hughes, Joe Haldeman, Gwyneth

Jones, and many more turn their imaginations to the wet and swampy Venus that Bradbury wrote about before the space probes gave a more realistic picture of the planet.

- George Orwell's *1984*, published in 1949, is a futuristic dystopia in which citizens are spied on and have no privacy. It summarizes all the fears of World War II with its totalitarian and fascist regimes. The novel is more relevant than ever with publicity about current government surveillance programs that seem to fulfill the novel's slogan, "Big Brother is watching you."

- Carl Sagan's *Cosmos: A Personal Voyage* was a 1980 television series and best-selling book that made space exploration an exciting reality to large audiences. Sagan was a friend of Bradbury's and wrote his own science fiction novel, *Contact* (1985). *Cosmos* is rewarding to watch and read because of Sagan's enthusiasm for finding extraterrestrial life in the universe. The fourth episode explains the difference between Old Venus and New Venus. The book was updated in 2013 by Ann Druyan, Sagan's widow and coauthor. The foreword is by Neil deGrasse Tyson, the astrophysicist who inherited Sagan's mantle and television series.

- The 2016 best-selling book and film *Hidden Figures: The American Dream and the Untold Story of the Black Women Mathematicians Who Helped with the Space Race*, by Margot Lee Shetterly, tells of the pioneer efforts of the African American woman mathematicians who helped NASA in the space race using only slide rules and adding machines in the days before computers to calculate parameters such as the orbits of rockets. The book is available in a young reader edition.

Sources

Blish, James [William Atheling Jr.], *The Issue at Hand*, Advent Publishers, 1964, p. 48.

Bradbury, Ray, "All Summer in a Day," in *A Medicine for Melancholy and Other Stories*, Perennial, Harper Collins, 1990, pp. 88-93.

————, *Dandelion Wine*, William Morrow Reprint, 2006, pp. 10-11.

Drassinower, Abraham, and Cheryl Kemkow, "Ray Bradbury: An Interview," in *Conversations with Ray Bradbury*, edited by StevenL.Aggelis, University of Mississippi Press, 2004, pp. 112-21.

Eller, Jonathan R., and William F. Touponce, *Ray Bradbury: The Life of Fiction*, Kent State University Press, 2004, pp. 2-20, 375-76.

Isherwood, Christopher, Review of *The Martian Chronicles*, in *Tomorrow*, October 1950, pp. 56-58.

Kelley, Ken, *"Playboy* Interview: Ray Bradbury," in *Conversations with Ray Bradbury*, edited by Steven L. Aggelis, University of Mississippi Press, 2004, p. 154.

Knight, Damon, *In Search of Wonder: Essays on Modern Science Fiction*, Advent Publishers, 1956.

Mogen, David, *Ray Bradbury*, Twayne's United States Authors Series, No. 504, Twayne Publishers, 1986, pp. 1-5, 63-64, 73, 81, 85, 94.

Piantadosi, Claude A., *Mankind beyond Earth: The History, Science, and Future of Space Exploration*, Columbia University Press, 2012, pp. 7, 14-25, 85, 189, 242.

Prescott, Orville, Review of *Fahrenheit* 451, in *Ray Bradbury*, edited by David Mogen, Twayne's United States Authors Series, No. 504, Twayne Publishers, 1986, p. 16.

Priestley, J. B., "They Came from Inner Space," in *New Statesman and Nation*, Vol. 46, December 5, 1953, p. 712.

Reid, Robin Anne, *Ray Bradbury: A Critical Companion*, Greenwood Press, 2000, pp. 63, 71, 75, 83.

Roberts, Adam, *The History of Science Fiction*, Palgrave Macmillan, 2006, p. 218.

Unger, Arthur, "Ray Bradbury: The Science of Science Fiction," in *Conversations with Ray Bradbury*, edited by Steven L. Aggelis, University of Mississippi Press, 2004, pp. 107–12.

Weller, Sam, *Listen to the Echoes: The Ray Bradbury Interviews*, Melville House Publishing, 2010, pp. 108, 115.

Wilson, Angus, Review of *Fahrenheit 451*, in *Science Fiction News*, May/June 1953, p. 2.

Wood, Edward, "The Case Against Ray Bradbury," in *Journal of Science Fiction*, Vol. 1, No. 1, Fall 1951, pp. 8–12.

Further Reading

Bradbury, Ray, *Zen in the Art of Writing*, Capra Press, 1990.

> This is Bradbury's impressive collection of essays on the creative process and tips that he passes on to other writers.

Le Guin, Ursula, *The Dispossessed*, 1974.

> This is the fifth novel of the Hainish cycle, in which Le Guin pictures structures of life on various planets as speculative anthropological experiments. This is an anarchist utopian novel about the fictional twin planets of Urras and Anarres. Le Guin, a postmodern science fiction writer treating feminist, environmental, and political ideas, has won the Grandmaster Award for Science Fiction, and this book won the Nebula, Hugo, and Locus awards.

Seed, David, *Ray Bradbury: Modern Masters of Science Fiction Series*, University of Illinois Press, 2015.

> This excellent critical study follows Bradbury's beginnings in the science fiction pulp magazines and devotes

major attention to his two most
notable science fiction works, *The
Martian Chronicles* and *Fahrenheit
451*. There is also a chapter on
Bradbury's religious ideas about
space travel.

Weller, Sam, *The Bradbury Chronicles: The Life of
Ray Bradbury*, Harper Collins, 2005.

Weller is a journalist who was a fan
and friend of Bradbury's and spent
many hours interviewing him and
gathering materials.

Suggested Search Terms

Ray Bradbury

"All Summer in a Day" AND Bradbury

space exploration

NASA

Venus exploration

science fiction

fantasy

science fiction AND film

Carl Sagan AND Cosmos

female science fiction writers